Overcome Betrayal:

How to rebuild trust and live with joy and fulfillment

Hélène Patry

Patry, Hélène
Overcome Betrayal: How to rebuild trust and live with joy and fulfillment / Hélène Patry - 1st ed.
Book 3 of the "Overcome" Series.
First Edition: August 2015
ISBN-13: 978-1515331674

Other titles:
Overcome Perfectionism: How to find joy in what you do and have healthier relationships / Hélène Patry - 1st ed. Book 2 of the "Overcome" Series. First Edition: Jun 2015

Overcome Being Bullied: A proven step-by-step system to boost self-esteem, release anxiety and restore health if you were bullied by a sibling, an adult, or at school / Hélène Patry - 1st ed. Book 1 of the "Overcome" Series. First Edition: May 2015

Contact information:
Website: http://www.HelenePatry.com
Email: Helene@HelenePatry.com
Facebook: http://www.Facebook.com/HelenePatry747

DEDICATION

This book is dedicated
to
Life, in all its wonders.
May it continue to lead us
To the answers we seek,
The joys we want,
The love we all deserve.

CONTENTS

1 INTRODUCTION

If you are like most people, you would love to improve your self-esteem and find happiness along with loving relationships. The key is within you, and only you have the power to open that door. The ideas in this book strive to provide you with the tools you need to release what is holding you back so you can finally feel that contentment, that excitement for tomorrow.

It was my own search for physical health that led me on this journey. Over ten years ago, I left a life-long career in high technology to find answers for my deteriorating health that no one could diagnose. I turned to Energy Medicine and became a practitioner. Along the way, my intuition flourished, and it allowed me to start seeing what was lying behind the physical ailments that were besetting my clients. After ten years of doing this work, it's been my experience that the vast majority of what happens to us, whether in our bodies, our relationships or our businesses, is connected to events in the past. These events either left some trauma, a belief or an association that became hard-coded into our very bodies. And when we want to heal a part of our life, it's more effective if we first understand how the issue was created in the first place, and then to release the emotional charge connected to the event, thereby returning us to a more natural state of being.

The research that I've done has been a compendium of reading, countless teleseminars and the personal experience of my clients, myself being one of them! So please understand that I hold no degree that is officially recognized by the medical community. As such, you are reading this material for your own information, and you choose what makes sense to you. You are advised to seek the advice of the appropriate medical practitioner before you apply the suggested techniques. I can only tell you that I've witnessed spontaneous recoveries, and complete transformations in people's lives when they change the way they understand events and then clear the trauma from their cells.

As cliché as this may sound, most of what appears to impact us in our adult life has an origin in childhood. When we are very young, we can't make sense of what's happening so we react in very intense and sometimes confused ways. We depend on others to show us the way, and if those others somehow don't fulfill our every need, we start feeling insecure, that this is not a safe place to be.

Our need for safety is at the very base of our most intense reactions, because it stems from a compulsion towards survival that dates back to cave days and that still resides in our amygdala. Back then, we needed to be part of a tribe in order to survive. We increased our odds of remaining in the tribe if we were loved. So the need to be loved became as intense as the impulse to survive. Which led us to the behaviors that try to fulfill that very important need.

There seem to be three aspects that can lead us to either feel safe and loved, or the opposite. Think of it as a three-legged stool. If any leg is damaged or missing, then we might not be able to sit and enjoy the scenery. We would be constantly trying to compensate for the imbalance that this defective stool causes.

The vast majority of people that I've met in my life have had at least one of these "stool legs" go wobbly. The three legs are established in childhood and consist of:

- Feeling that we are accepted as we are.
- Feeling that our parents/caretakers are there for us and want to be with us.
- Feeling that there is an order to life that we can understand and rely on.

If the first leg is defective, it will generally be because we have been repeatedly criticized, teased or abused when we were young. This could have come from sibling rivalry, a critical or overbearing parent, at school, or from any other person who held some form of authority over us. This kind of treatment would have led us to believe that there was something wrong with us, and we carried this belief into adulthood. It would affect almost every part of our life until we released it. Restoring the stability to this leg is the subject of my first book, "*Overcome Being Bullied*".

If the second leg is flawed, then we probably felt abandoned at some point in childhood, and many people can point to several instances of feeling abandoned. This tends to lead us to believe that we had somehow done something wrong, and that we needed to "do" better in order to regain the attention of the absent caregiver. The absence can be physical or emotional, such as a parent who is too preoccupied by other matters in their life to tend to the emotional needs of their child. Returning to a state of balance on this leg is the topic of my second book, "*Overcome Perfectionism*".

The topic of this third book deals with what to do if we've felt betrayed. Betrayal is a strong word, but it's appropriate when we consider the immense needs of a child. Very few parents are able to fully recognize, let alone meet, all of the child's points of possible insecurity with unconditional love and attention. After all, when in utero, the child's needs are always met, and always immediately, barring severe circumstances in the mother's life. In fact, I'm not even sure that the child feels any needs, since it's being fed and kept warm and safe at all times.

When we were born, suddenly many of our needs were no longer met at once. Expressing our discomfort through crying normally brought relief and a return to contentment. We were entirely dependent on our caregivers for survival, so having our needs met by them was critical. If this pattern of our needs being met continued, then we developed a strong sense that the world was a safe place, from which we could start exploring our surroundings and gain proficiency with our fingers and toes. We then learned more about the world, that a hot oven could mean ouch, bath bubbles were fun, finishing a meal earned approval, and there was a certain order to things (each day included waking, eating, playing, bath time, and sleep). Above all, we knew that there was always someone nearby to run to if we needed them.

But what about when this idyllic scenario is altered? Here are four categories of events that can lead someone to feeling that the world is not a safe place:

1. We had a parent or caregiver that was critical of us. We felt that we could only earn their love by behaving according to their standards. And sometimes those standards were erratic.

2. We had a parent or caregiver who left us in some way, whether voluntarily or involuntarily such as through death or illness; or our parent didn't have time for us, didn't pay attention to us the way we wanted, or we felt in their way.

3. Our parent treated us differently than our other siblings, or differently than the relationship we saw between our friends and their parents.

4. Our parent didn't protect us. We were hurting in some way and our parent didn't interfere and come to our rescue. Examples include allowing our siblings to bully us, or not believing us when we complained of an adult mistreating us.

In all cases, what this boils down to is that we believed that our parent had a role, and they didn't fulfill that role so we felt cheated. Their role is an implied promise, and if they broke that promise, then we could have felt betrayed. For the purposes of this book, I define betrayal as the breaking of a promise, whether implied or explicit. And for a child who is entirely dependent, both physically and emotionally, on the care, love, attention and guidance of their parents, this perceived betrayal leaves an imprint in the subconscious mind.

Thereafter, our subconscious mind, which has our survival and protection as its primary imperatives, will be forever watchful of possible future betrayal. The more we look for the color blue, the more we find the color blue. And the more we are watchful for something we fear, the more we end up attracting it in our life. So it's our job to return to the scene of the original belief and heal it there, as well as the other instances of betrayal we may have experienced in our life.

We need to change how we perceive events. Betrayal is no different. Yes, we truly felt it, it was very real to us and it had a huge impact on our life. As a matter of fact, we can easily point to cases where betrayal was done overtly. But that's not the point. The issue is that we want to restore our faith that we can enjoy personal relationships with people and that how we feel about ourselves won't depend on their actions and choices.

And that is the goal of this book. You deserve full happiness. It's possible for you. And it doesn't require perfect circumstances. What it does require is a choice. Throughout these pages, you'll be invited to release the pain, and that includes the resentment you feel towards those who have betrayed you. Give yourself the time you need, but do read on. Imagine how wonderful it will be to not be triggered anymore by this crazy human construct! We act in strange ways when we are caught up in our own drama. It's time for us to change the game. Yay!

2 INTRODUCTION TO ENERGY MEDICINE

[This chapter is taken from my previous book, Overcome Being Bullied. You can skip it if you've read it before.]

We all know that stress affects your health. As a matter of fact, every thought and emotion you have releases a flood of hormones and chemicals in your body. This happens whether the situation is real or vividly imagined. For example, someone who has a phobia of spiders may start sweating at the mere thought of spiders, even if there are none present. If you're nervous about an upcoming interview, you may find your stomach clenching. If you're in love, your heart may feel like it will burst. If you're feeling angry because you're stuck in traffic that will cause you to be late, you might feel as if your blood is boiling. If you're feeling embarrassed, you may blush. These are all physical consequences of mere thoughts, and it's more our reaction and interpretation than the actual event that is precipitating the emotion connected to the thought. In the example above of spiders, you can have a phobia, or you can be fascinated by all their different colors and the complexity of their webs.

The beliefs we have planted into our subconscious mind tend to cause us to go into broken-record thought patterns that recreate the physical cascade of consequences over and over again. If we repeat this pattern often enough, these chemicals can accumulate and create a disruption in our system.

Energy medicine is founded on the premise that everything is energy, and energy works best when it flows freely. Even physicists have discovered that the core of matter consists of nothing but quickly vibrating "strings". You have various systems of energy coursing through your body, and one of the best-known is the meridian system. The meridians are energy pathways linking different parts of your body, each one connecting to one or more organs. Chinese acupuncture is based on ensuring that the flow of energy is restored along the meridians to assist your body to return to proper balance and health. This can help relieve psychological stress and physical pain.

Meridian Tapping

Meridian tapping is a form of psychological acupressure that uses a gentle tapping with fingertips instead of needles to stimulate traditional acupuncture points. The tapping on the designated points is combined with verbalizing as detailed below. Originally called EFT (Emotional Freedom Technique), it was developed in the early 1990s by Gary Craig, who has seen it grow and applied to every kind of physical and emotional issue since.

Tapping is one of the techniques that we will use as it's easy to learn and you can perform it on yourself. It consists of a setup phrase that is repeated 3 times, then guides you to tap through 8 meridian points on the face and body while repeating the issue first and then new choices. The points are mirrored and you can choose either side (for example, either the left or right side of the face).

Here are the tapping points:

Karate chop point: for the setup phrase, tap with 3 fingers of the opposite hand on the side of the hand, where your hand would hit an object if you were to perform a karate chop.

Eyebrow: the beginning of the eyebrow, close to the nose, right on the bone

Side of the eye: the bone just to the outside of the eye

Under the eye: the bone immediately below the eye

Under the nose: between the nose and lip, right in the middle

Chin: just below the mouth, in the middle of the chin where the indentation is

Collar bone: the indentation just below and outside of the collar bone. To make is easier, just tap with all fingers flat on the area where a man's tie would be

Under the arm: about 4 inches below the armpit, right where a woman's bra would be

Top of the head: right on the crown of the head. Some people prefer to tap around the area to make sure they hit the spot.

You will get the greatest benefit from this technique if you are completely focused on the issue you're addressing and really feeling the feelings. Please understand that you are not reinforcing the negative feelings when you say them out loud: you are finally giving them a voice and the simultaneous tapping is allowing the energy that was blocked in your body related to that feeling to finally start moving. You'll feel a great deal of relief at finally being able to be completely honest with yourself.

Please see a video demonstration of the tapping technique at: http://www.HelenePatry.com/Tapping.htm

Visualization

There are many practical tools and techniques that can be of tremendous help and I use them regularly. Just like brushing your teeth is something you have to do every day, ensuring your energy system is flowing properly also deserves your regular attention. Most of these tools involve some form of visualization. Here is an example to get you started. Most people find it easier to visualize with their eyes closed.

Imagine you are standing under a large shower head. Turn on the faucet and instead of water, see a flow of light coming out and flowing over you. Allow this light to gently flow through you, and wash away any worry and tension you may have. This light flows all the way down to your feet, and the light carries all of the stress down, down the drain. Let this light cleanse you for as long as you wish. You will feel immediately better after doing this.

Your imagination is a very powerful tool. You can use it in ways that help you or ways that hurt you, such as imagining undesired outcomes. Please choose to use your imagination to benefit you and you can experience what a powerful creator you are.

3 THE SOURCE

Understanding that betrayal was the basic issue of the third leg of the foundational stool came as a surprise to me. I knew that it existed, but didn't realize how pervasive it was until more recently.

Betrayal is certainly not an emotion that can be identified or recognized at an early age. I believe that the feeling develops over time as a result of the many ways we discover that life doesn't always work out the way we think it should.

For example, when we see a television show such as "Leave It to Beaver", we can see that what is portrayed is not what we are experiencing. Expressions like "I love her like a sister" are really confusing to those whose sibling rivalry reached epic proportions.

When life suddenly becomes "work", at least in part, then we may feel disillusioned about life in general. This can take place when we are given new responsibilities such as chores, or are expected to become responsible and independent because our parents have new commitments that reduce how much attention they can direct to us. If there is a growing or sudden lack of feeling safe, then life doesn't feel as good anymore. This can happen if a parent loses a job so that money becomes an issue, a tragedy in the home or to a member of the family, or a jarring event in a parent's life that can leave them emotionally unable to care for us, their children.

If we express a pain but we feel dismissed because it's not accorded the right degree of seriousness, then we begin to believe that how we feel is not considered important. We may start to dismiss our feelings as well, since that's the pattern we are "taught" to model. And since how we feel is the most accurate barometer of what is going on inside us, we end up losing touch with the core of who we are and what drives us to make the choices that we do. Finally, feeling unimportant is the most egregious way that we can feel cheated of experiencing the best that life has to offer.

What I believe sets us up for believing that life should be a certain way is how our entire society is governed by different sets of rules. Consider:

- Governmental laws, from federal down to municipal. Some of us even have laws that govern our own neighborhood, in the form of HOA guidelines (Home Owner's Association).

- Religious edicts. If we want to have a happy Everafter, then we need to behave according to certain dictates.

- Schools establish rules of conduct and standards of learning. We must sit at our desk, do the homework and pass the tests.

- The home carries its own set of rules set by the parents. Different homes may have different rules (curfew, for example), but most homes have a standard set of categories for which they establish rules.

- Games come with rules that we must follow in order to win.

- Even personal relationships have, if not rules, at least principles that should be followed to boost chances of success.

- Sometimes local customs define the rules of the game. For example, even in countries where we're driving on the same side of the road, navigating streets and highways in Montreal, Canada; Rome, Italy; and Georgetown, Indiana, are very different adventures!

Rules are an important aspect of a smoothly-running society. If everyone behaves according to the rules, then we have a systematic pattern on which we can depend. And it helps us establish expectations. If we follow a rule then we're likely to get a predictable outcome. Without a clear set of rules, things can be a little chaotic.

This is where life throws in a wrench. This picture isn't actual reality! It's a target and a hope, and for the most part it behaves reasonably well. The structure may be a little limiting, but we need it so that at least some of our decisions are made for us. It would be exhausting to have to decide what to do at every intersection of the roads we're traveling without some basic traffic laws.

Rules and structure provide us with a sense or order, of safety. When someone breaks a rule, we can feel "blindsided" and get as sense of "Hey!", like when someone runs a red light, cutting us off. In that particular instance, once our heart rate goes back to normal, we probably feel a little offended that the other driver didn't show us the courtesy of following the rule, but for the most part, we may not take it too personally and it's fairly easy to let it go.

However, if the other car hit us in that scenario, then the consequences of the rule-breaking are more serious. Not only do we need to tend to car and body, but our sense of order has been unsettled. If someone can choose to not follow the rules and we end up as the victim, then the world doesn't feel like such a safe place anymore. It may be subtle, but we may feel a little betrayed by "Life". After all, Life said follow the rules and things will turn out OK.

One such instance will shake us, but having other occurrences of various types of betrayal can accumulate and generate anger and disillusionment.

Most of us had needs that weren't fully met as children. We formed an illusion that Life played by a set of rules like everything else. We were supposed to be taken care of when we were little. If that didn't happen from our perspective, then we felt like Life didn't deliver on its promise, and a sense of unease about our ability to trust Life set in. But the only option we had was to proceed, and when we met further instances of what felt like betrayal, our sense of a reliable foundation grew increasingly shaky.

There are no guarantees in life. Consider Jim Fixx, an author with substantial influence in the fitness industry in the late 1970s. He died at age 52 while jogging. Conversely, you've probably heard of people who lived into their 90s on a diet of meat and potatoes. Where's the fairness??

Some, if not most, of our judgments about fairness are based on an incomplete picture of reality. Someone following a strictly organic diet and a well-balanced exercise regimen can still be ill. Ridiculous stress can cause this, as can other emotional burdens, for example. Maybe someone has a genetic predisposition that their lifestyle didn't alter. Maybe the events of today, as uncomfortable as they feel in the present, are setting us up perfectly for a glorious scenario in the future.

You may have heard of the fable of the old farmer. The details change every time I hear this story, but the point remains the same. An old man lived on his farm with his son. They had a horse that the son loved dearly. One day, the horse ran away. Neighbors decried that this was bad. But the next day, the horse returned with a mare in tow and they stayed together. Neighbors judged this as good. When the farmer's son was trying to tame the mare, he fell and broke his leg. "Bad", was the conclusion. But the next day, the army came by to enlist young men in a war. Since the son had a broken leg, he couldn't join. "Good", said the neighbors.

So how can we judge? We believe we have a clear picture in the moment. But if we expand our view, in time and/or in space, we get a different perspective, one which is not always available to us when we want it. The example above shows us that looking over a larger time span gives the events a new interpretation. "In space" means looking at how different people and circumstances are intertwined, allowing us a new overall understanding.

So coming back to the topic at hand, we need to release our perspective on the set of rules by which Life plays. If we swerve into oncoming traffic to avoid a child who just ran into the street, then technically we broke a rule, but we probably did the right thing. Let's grant Life similar leeway. If something doesn't make sense to us, let's do the best we can with what we have, and accept the fact that there are aspects that we can't see at present.

As it applies to our perception that Life has somehow cheated us, that Life owes us happiness if we follow the rules, let's completely turn that on its head.

If we feel that we didn't get what we needed as children, then we might blame our parents. After all, our parents were the ones responsible for ushering us safely into independence. Instead, we may have adopted behavior patterns that tried to compensate for the low self-esteem that arose from feeling mistreated in some way. And because our life choices resulted from our behaviors and beliefs adopted in childhood, we can end up pointing the finger at our parents for all of the ways in which our lives didn't turn out how we wanted.

The mind seeks order. And holding our parents responsible for our unhappiness satisfies the ego's need to be righteous. But it's time to take responsibility for ourselves. It's time to see that it would have been almost impossible for our parents to be perfect, to have no emotional baggage of their own, to always have time, energy and patience for us, to guess at every turn exactly what we needed and be equipped to give it to us. It's time to realize that even though our hurts were very real, that they may have created beliefs that were based on incomplete information. It's time for us to take back ownership for our choices, move into the present, and recognize that the past may have shaped us, but we get to be the sculptor from now on. It's time to release the past to give us the space we need to unleash the future.

Part one is to address the feeling that we were cheated out of being fully loved in childhood.

Karate chop point: 1. Even though I didn't get the safety and love I wanted when I was a child, I deeply and completely understand that I can manage my own needs now.
2. Even though I really wish my parents had acted differently when I was young, I deeply and completely accept that they were imperfect just like everyone else.
3. Even though I don't think it's fair that I didn't get what I needed when I was little, I deeply and completely recognize that I drew conclusions without seeing the full picture.

Eyebrow: It really hurt
Side of the eye: I really wanted all their love
Under the eye: I really needed all their love
Under the nose: When I didn't have their attention, I felt unsafe
Chin: I felt so alone sometimes
Collarbone: I felt like they didn't understand me

Under the arm: I felt like they didn't have enough time for me
Top of the head: And that made me feel really unsure of myself

Eyebrow: Lately I've been feeling that it wasn't fair
Side of the eye: I should have gotten more love
Under the eye: I should have gotten more attention
Under the nose: I should have been the apple of their eyes
Chin: I should have been better taken care of
Collarbone: I should have been recognized as vulnerable
Under the arm: And they should have known what I needed
Top of the head: They should have given me more

Eyebrow: I really wish things had been different
Side of the eye: It would be so much easier on me now
Under the eye: I wouldn't have adopted all those bad beliefs about myself
Under the nose: I wouldn't have believed there was something unlovable about me
Chin: I would have felt more important
Collarbone: And it would have given me more courage
Under the arm: To claim what I want from Life
Top of the head: To be everything that I could be

Eyebrow: But instead I stayed a reduced "me"
Side of the eye: Because I never felt good enough
Under the eye: I feel so betrayed by Life
Under the nose: It shouldn't have been this way
Chin: It's not supposed to be this way
Collarbone: I'm so angry that this happened to me

Under the arm: It just isn't fair
Top of the head: I was too young to understand

Eyebrow: But now I'm not as young anymore
Side of the eye: And I have a better idea
Under the eye: A new idea on how things probably were
Under the nose: And though I felt very affected by them
Chin: Though I had very real fears and disappointments
Collarbone: I'm willing to look at things differently now
Under the arm: And see how my parents probably weren't to blame
Top of the head: They did what they could and I'm the one who decided it wasn't enough

Take a deep breath.

Part two of the foundational beliefs comes from the idea that we were cheated by Life because it's not playing by the rules that we were taught. We think that if people play by the rules, they tell the truth and keep their promises.

We can probably think of a list of people whom we believe have betrayed us to varying degrees throughout our lives. Why is this happening? My understanding of how Life works is that it "conspires" to bring to us exactly what we need to release false beliefs about ourselves. Actually, it's not so much "Life" that does it rather than our own soul crying for freedom, but it's easier to say Life!

So what is the false belief? Every time something happens "to" us, we must turn it around and recognize that it is merely a mirror for what we are doing ourselves. I believe the logic is as follows. We somehow come to believe that we are not good enough as we are, because we're not getting all the love an attention that we want. So it must be our fault. We try to *be* and *do* better, in the hopes or receiving the love we need, and this may work sometimes. We attempt to adapt to how we believe the other person wants us to behave, and so we end up taking on a role. Some feelings are not appreciated and cause people to move away from us, so we push those feelings down or try to pretend they don't exist.

And in playing this role, in pretending that everything's OK when it's not, in going along with someone else's choice when we don't even express our preference out of fear of meeting with disapproval,

... we betray ourselves.

No other form of lying, cheating or breaking the rules can top the fact that by betraying ourselves, we are actually giving permission to others to betray us too. We are declaring to the universe that we are not OK, that we are somehow flawed, even though deep down what we really want is for someone to convince us otherwise. But no one can dig us out of that hole we have created for ourselves, because, unbeknownst to us, our primary belief can't be overturned by anyone other than those we consider to have planted it there. That is, if our own parents, the human beings who adore us more than anyone else in the world, can't even love us enough to give us the reassurance that we are OK, then no one else will be able to. There *must* be something wrong with us. No amount of compliments or achievements will be able to convince us otherwise.

Let's tap this out, because now that we understand it, we can release it.

Karate chop point: 1. Even though I'm convinced that I'm not completely lovable, I deeply and completely know that I'm ready to change that belief now.
2. Even though I've always thought there was something wrong with me, I deeply and completely allow myself to see things differently now.
3. Even though I never seemed to feel good about myself for long, I deeply and completely choose that this is changing today!

Eyebrow: I thought it was other people betraying me
Side of the eye: I was so angry at them for what they did
Under the eye: I was counting on them and they let me down
Under the nose: I believed them when they promised me but they didn't follow through
Chin: I thought they didn't love me enough to honor their commitments
Collarbone: And I was so angry at them for the things they did to me
Under the arm: I felt awful about myself as a result
Top of the head: And I just wanted to blame them for it

Eyebrow: But now I understand that I'm the one who attracted them in my life
Side of the eye: So that I could finally see that betrayal started with me
Under the eye: With the fact that I betrayed myself by not allowing me to be me
Under the nose: By thinking that there was something wrong with me

Chin: I really did get those beliefs honestly
Collarbone: I didn't do it on purpose to take on those thoughts
Under the arm: But it's what happened
Top of the head: And as a result, I thought I couldn't be fully me

Eyebrow: It's OK to me be
Side of the eye: Actually, it's more than OK
Under the eye: I need to be me
Under the nose: So that I can grow and explore what else is out there
Chin: It takes too much energy to hide the real me
Collarbone: Too much energy and too much anxiety
Under the arm: Anxiety at the thought that someone would find me out
Top of the head: But now they can because I've decided to be me!

Eyebrow: I've decided that it's time for me
Side of the eye: The real me to come out of hiding
Under the eye: It's time to acknowledge all parts of me
Under the nose: I'll be more loving to others
Chin: By sharing with them the way I truly feel
Collarbone: Because there's no stuffing down what I really feel
Under the arm: I get to be gentle in my honesty when I express myself
Top of the head: Because now I give myself permission to be me
Eyebrow: I was trying to hide from myself
Side of the eye: But there's no hiding anymore
Under the eye: I may be flawed but at least I'm real
Under the nose: And by letting go the need to be perfect

Chin: I can meet other people where they are too
Collarbone: And we can let go of the judgments from the past
Under the arm: That said it wasn't OK to be us
Top of the head: Because now I give myself full permission to be me

Take a deep breath.

4 WHAT OUR PARENTS DIDN'T TEACH US

Now that we know where the entire concept of betrayal comes from, let's explore more the instances that we've experienced in a new light. These examinations should be easier now that we know what was at their root. Let's start with looking at how we might have perceived our parents didn't fulfilling their entire role. As discussed before, we've covered how they may have made us feel criticized or abandoned, topics well covered in my first two books. Here, we drill down into how we felt they didn't prepare us properly for life. Technically, this boils down to what they didn't teach us.

1. Money management.
    a - The basics of earning, saving and spending.
    b - Career options and planning. Entrepreneurship.
    c - Investing.
    d - Retirement planning.
    e - How to think about wealthy people.
2. Health management.
    a - Basic nutrition.
    b - Preparing food.
    c - Sports and activities.
    d - Health care options.

3. Taking responsibility.
   a - Choices and consequences.
   b - Honoring commitments.
   c - The buck stops here.
   d - Caring for the environment.
4. Personal interactions.
   a - Listening.
   b - Teamwork.
   c - Honoring differences.
   d - Understanding the existence of different countries
and cultures.
5. Relationships and roles.
   a - Evolving relationships physically and emotionally.
   b - Establishing roles and boundaries.
   c - Keeping communications open.
6. Learning to think and discern.
   a - Researching.
   b - Evaluating information.
7. Exposure to technology and its role in the world.

Fill in whatever other category that you feel belongs to this list. Some of the things that parents didn't teach us are due to:
- Lack of time or energy. It takes so much longer to teach a child something than to do it themselves.
- Expecting that the school would teach it.
- Lack of knowledge in the subject matter or a personal issue with the topic.
- Not realizing the importance of actually teaching the child the topic.
- Inability to predict what the child will face in coming years.

Apart from this mini-outline on parenting suggestions, parents were often teaching us by example rather than explicitly. And if the family environment was somehow dysfunctional, then what we learned as children could confuse our efforts to have a successful family of our own in the future.

For example, if overt criticism wasn't highlighted as unacceptable when we grew up, then we may find ourselves in relationships in the future where we are criticized or we criticize our partner. After all, that's how we behave in a family, so it rolls off the tongue effortlessly, even if we don't actually enjoy that dynamic.

Another example is how our parents dealt with finances. If we saw worry, liberal spending, etc, it will affect how we interact with money as well. Changing those patterns later in life requires us to go back to the source, as we are doing here for betrayal.

One of the fascinating aspects of what we failed to learn as a child can bleed into our perception of the parental roles themselves. For example, if our mother did all the cooking and never taught us to cook, we will start our independent life fumbling around the kitchen and either not take care of ourselves nutritionally, or learn to cook by ourselves, maybe starting with our family recipes. Some people quite enjoy the process of cooking, but others end up not really wanting to take on the task.

Some of the resentment could be attached to a subconscious refusal to step into adulthood fully: "She didn't teach me to cook; it's not my job; if I learn to do it I'll show myself even more independent and I'll be separated from her even more; I still need her to take care of me a little".

Another aspect is the possible rejection of the entire housewife role. Some cultures revere the mother's place in the household, but others have judged business achievements as more laudable than domestic duties. If we felt this inequality between parents, then we may have decided that being a housewife didn't garner the respect and attention that we wanted so we would want to distance ourselves from it. To our eyes, the role consisted of repetitive and less worldly chores. The role was basically subordinate to the father, since his career dictated the location and circumstances and the mother had to adapt. The mother's world tended to revolve around the needs of her family, she was completely dependent on the father financially, and her ability to make decisions appeared very limited. She was so busy taking care of the practical part of running a household that she didn't have as much time for us as we wanted.

For any or all of these reasons, we may have decided that we didn't want to step into the housewife role. As such, we may also have ended up painting all aspects of the role with the same brush, and essentially thrown out the baby with the bathwater. Meaning that instead of ending up being stubbornly against the idea of cooking, we could look at what aspects of the role we consciously believe serve us and decide to take those on willingly and joyfully.

Finally, if we judged the role (not the person) as boring, we could have decided that most aspects of the role could be hired out, so the role didn't "matter" very much. This would be more the case if we didn't feel a deep connection with the person in the role.

So if that role didn't matter, what actually *does* matter? What could be more important than taking beautiful babies and helping them launch into the wealth of possibilities that life has to offer?

Why not make up your own list of what you believe really matters? Regardless of how someone else might answer, it's important to realize what you consider important. The next page contains the list that I created.

What matters:
1.
2.
3.
.
.
.

The things that I consider important are:

- Making someone smile.
- Providing insights for someone so that they can solve a problem and move forward.
- Making someone feel special.
- Doing something for someone so they experience joy and/or pleasure.
- Hearing laughter.
- Caring for those I love.
- Showing compassion.
- Accepting people as they are.
- Finding solutions to problems.
- Giving myself what I need.
- Considering myself important enough to take care of myself.
- Honoring myself with the gift of beauty (such as flowers).
- Balancing my needs with other people's needs of me.
- Building community.
- Spreading joy and hope.
- Making a commitment to something or someone I really care about.
- Giving people the space to be who they are (including me).
- Honoring others for what they have become and have accomplished.
- Accepting that people have different points of view.

Money

If our parents didn't teach us about long-term money management, it may be because they were of the generation (for many of us, anyway!) where they went to work for a large corporation, they worked for that same company their entire career, and the company funded their retirement. This scenario no longer exists, except in very few cases such as the federal government. Most Americans soon facing retirement have less than $50,000 saved. They are dependent on government programs, such as social security and Medicare, in order to meet their financial obligations. Since these may be insufficient, the retiree needs to look for other solutions, and actual retirement may not offer them the freedom they expected.

Although there are potential avenues to generate additional income at this stage, what we want to look at here is another very pointed situation where we may feel that we were ill prepared. We need someone to take care of us, as our parents did when we were young and not expected to earn a living. We come to expect a reward after having achieved a particular task. Even a meal carries the "eat your vegetables then you can have dessert" conditioning. So after a lifetime of devoting ourselves to living according to the rules and attend to a job for decades, we expect the promised reward of a leisure-filled retirement when we can finally relax.

Part of the problem with this scenario is that, just like with the vegetables we hadn't learned to love yet, the "work" part becomes a chore, just to be endured until we can get the "reward". Seventy percent of Americans don't enjoy their job. How can that possibly produce a happy society? We come to believe that our options are limited, that we need to stay in a job where we have gained some competency or we have invested heavily in the pertinent education, and that we are basically "stuck" there. We don't think we have the time, energy, money, or even permission to venture somewhere else from a career standpoint. Even more problematic is the fact that we would have to start from scratch in a new field, and that would be very hard on our ego, which wants us to feel proficient and superior.

If this is in large part an ego issue, let's see where the ego and the feeling of betrayal connect.

The ego wants to ensure survival.

==> Survival means having the means to obtain everything we need (usually translated as "money"), and having a tribe to help protect us from unpredictable outside forces or harm (illness, natural disaster, accident, political instability).

==> Making money means we have to have skills that are judged as worth paying for, and we need to have enough visibility and recognition within the community to find those that will pay us that money. If we have been raised in an environment that emphasized competition, then we believe we need to show that we are better than others in order to get the job/contract/sale. And competition is bred into us at a very early age, since we feel we are constantly competing against other people and to-do lists for our parents' attention and love. If we win, then we get what we want and need. If we don't win, then the pain from missing that loving attention feels like a punishment.

==> So we come to believe that we need to top others in order to get the money / recognition / safety we need because we are convinced these resources are finite. The ego takes on the job of pushing us to feel we have won at least in some areas.

==> If we have found a job, and it meets at least our basic needs, then our ego may keep us there, not wanting to move because moving could threaten the survival that we have now. Unless we have a vast amount of faith in our own abilities to be successful somewhere else (that we might prefer), then fear may keep us where we are and we end up not enjoying it over the long run because we feel we have no choice.

==> There is a perverse belief that if we disdain something, then we are superior to it, such as a food critic that insists on superior fare in order to be satisfied. So if we stay in a job that we don't like, then not only are we declaring ourselves as superior to it, but we are not threatening the ego by looking elsewhere and feeling incompetent in that new position, even if just at the start.

==> The other aspect of staying in a job that we don't like is that we take on the martyr archetype. If we are suffering to put food on the table, then not only will our families not expect more from us because we are already to the point of pain, but there is an inherent honor in sacrificing yourself for the good of others. In actual martyrdom, the hero usually dies for his cause. He is venerated for his willingness to suffer, and his actions live on in history. He is guaranteed a special place in Heaven. So returning to our staying in a job that we don't like, by taking on the martyr archetype, we subconsciously expect the commensurate rewards. The ego wins, and we know things will be great at some point. The big difference here is that without knowing it, we think retirement is when the reward will be bestowed onto us (the end of the work like), and that illusion may come to a crashing halt when we get there. So we can feel completely betrayed by the implied promise of our choice.

So let's make sure that we have a sit-down with our ego, and that we decide what is truly better for us. Acting out of survival instinct may be necessary, but it's not much fun, and it shouldn't define our entire lives.

Health

Where health is concerned, there are too many variables for anyone to teach a child exactly what will work best. Not only does each individual thrive on a combination that may be somewhat different than for someone else, but a person's needs can change over time. As a foundation, however, recommending colorful fruits and vegetables, whole fresh foods, and a preference for organic is a pretty safe bet. So why aren't we doing more of it?

Two thirds of Americans are either overweight or obese. We are obviously not following the recommendations systematically. Some of the reasons for this include:
- We didn't learn about nutrition and its importance.
- We take our health for granted.
- We don't make the connection between our lifestyle choices and issues in the body.
- We are confused by contradictory scientific evidence.
- We don't take responsibility (such as suing McDonald's).

- We don't take the time and energy required to do it properly.
- We are unwilling to sacrifice - we want the rewards of food.

It's true that studies come out "proving" a theory, only to have other studies come later that disprove it. For example, we had the low-carb craze, followed by the low-fat movement, and we are now back to a low-carb recommendation. From the reading that I've done, the original low-carb diet was so full of saturated fat and too low on some other elements that your body needed that it wasn't entirely heart-healthy.

But the low-fat era actually saw obesity and diabetes rise considerably because of the commensurate rise in sugar-laden foods. Now evidence is pointing to carbs being the guilty party again, for everything from diabetes (because they cause too many sugar spikes, creating too-frequent insulin secretions, leading to insulin resistance in the cells which causes Type II diabetes), to Alzheimer's (which is also affected by insulin resistance in the brain), to gut microbiome issues (the "bad" microbes feed on sugar and starch and overrun the good guys, which are needed for proper digestion of nutrients and brain functioning), to weight gain (because those insulin spikes cause sugar to be stored as fat rather than burned for energy).

But what about those studies that show that very-low carbohydrate intake impairs your metabolism over the long run? Or other studies that show how ketones, which are released into your bloodstream as a result of fat cells breaking down from a low-carb food regimen, actually damage the brain? Argh!

Regardless of the current scientific preference, I think it must be pretty obvious that living on a diet of fast food is probably not what leads to long-term health. Or that super-sized portions are really a good idea. There are some basics that we could follow, so why don't we?

I believe that the main culprits are the last three items on the list above. First, for us to take responsibility means that we have to move into full adulthood, and there is some part of us that just doesn't want to grow up! Not the whole of us, of course. Most of us wouldn't welcome moving back into our original family home and abiding by all of the household rules again. We are far too independent for that. But we're never too old to want to be nurtured, to hand over the responsibilities just for a little while, to relinquish the need to be strong for everyone else around us even if only for an hour or two. It feels too hard to be responsible for everything. It feels unrelenting. And the easiest way to relent is in the area of food, because it appears so acceptable to do so.

It also does take extra time and energy to plan, shop for, prepare and clean up after a meal. The food industry has tried to automate some of the thinking with Meatless Mondays, Turkey Tuesdays, etc. But since it's a task that shows up every single day without fail, it can easily feel like too much work, especially when we have other responsibilities as well. There are tricks, such as being a weekend warrior cook, doing neighbor cooking exchanges (rotating who cooks for 3 families, say, and each family "owns" one night), or bulk cooking and freezing.

But the bottom line is that we need to consider this a priority, and a commitment. For someone who has betrayal issues, committing to anything can be a challenge. Let's explore that now.

Making a commitment means that we invest our time, energy and emotions into an endeavor. It means that we are willing to put our heart into something and believe that there will be particular benefits to doing so. It makes us vulnerable to some form of pain if the outcome doesn't materialize as expected. The pain could be lost time (and money if that was involved), disillusionment, lost hope, lost attachment to the idea of what the future was going to look like, and a hit to the ego because apparently we were wrong to have made that commitment after all. If we believe that Life has often not delivered on its promises, then we can be reluctant to expose ourselves to the pain of another broken promise. A commitment often implies several layers of promises. And a commitment to nourish ourselves properly is a promise that we make to ourselves, and we expect our lives and bodies to respond by improving.

The commitment may start with a surge of enthusiasm and faith. Faith that we can do it and faith that the outcome will be worth the effort. But unless the commitment is based on a deep-seated choice, then it relies on our willpower to sustain it. And willpower requires a lot of energy.

If we get sufficient positive feedback from our efforts in a short period of time, then that feeds the energy required to follow through. If the cycle continues successfully, then the new behavior can become a habit and the perception of the "cost" of carrying through is vastly diminished.

But what happens if despite our continued efforts, we are beset by a serious setback, such as an illness? Then all of that work, the commitment and the sacrifices that it entailed, all of it feels like it was a waste of time.

This feels like betrayal of the first order.

Why did this happen? Why are we being "punished" when we did what we thought was right, or at least what was expected of us? Why have we gone through all this just to fall flat on our face? Why do it? And most importantly, how can we believe in promises in the future? How can we bring ourselves to risk that great disappointment again?

Was it because we learned something?
Was it to show that there is more than one way to do something, that conventional wisdom is not always right, that we need to discern for ourselves?
Was it to teach us to follow more closely our own inner still small voice that we overrode with external rules?
Was it because this will lead to some great discovery?
Was it because it's causing us to encounter people and places that we would have otherwise never known?
Was it so that we would finally stop "running" and turn to introspection, something we normally would have avoided because it can be uncomfortable?
Or was it because this great failure is setting us up for our greatest triumph? That this failure is causing the breakdown of the entire structure of our false beliefs, allowing us to start all over again, building from truths? That this is the turning point in our lives when everything starts making sense?

What is a broken promise? It's our belief that something should turn out a certain way, and a completely different outcome hits us in the face instead. So what causes us to go and believe in the next promise? It's our giving away our power in the hopes of a particular reward later. It's our belief that something external holds the key to our happiness. It's our belief that we are somehow incomplete right here, right now. It's our attempt to find joy through some outcome in the future, rather than experiencing the joy in every step along the way *right now*.

Because if we experience the joy in every moment, then we won't judge the outcome so harshly. We will grant Life latitude for behaving according to some rules that we're not aware of yet. We will still feel that the endeavor was successful, because success means bringing into our lives what we consider important. And nothing is more important than feeling and sharing the joy of the moment. Let's remember our list of what matters. Let's integrate it into our lives, in every activity, and we have just created for ourselves a very successful life.

5 THE STRENGTH OF LOYALTY

Loyalty is one of those funny things - admired and expected, yet carried to extremes, it can be detrimental to someone's progress. Loyalty is essential in endeavors such as military exercises, where lives actually depend on the unity of the squadron, and the devotion of each of its members.

But when loyalty to someone is born out of the need for a consistent world view, then it can wreak havoc. For example, a woman I'll call Cathy had trouble in her small business. She said that no matter what she did, what promotion she ran, she always ended up with exactly the same revenue at the end of the month. It turns out that there was someone in her life that she looked up to, and she needed him to retain a status that was "above" her. If she had made more money than him, it would have somehow elevated her above him, and her sense of how things worked, her sense of order, would have been turned upside down. So by limiting her income, albeit completely subconsciously, her world could still make sense as it related to him.

Another example concerns "Isabel", who was so grateful for the loving sharing of knowledge from her teacher, that she limited her expansion to a level that would always be just below her teacher's. This was considered a form of respect in her culture, so she believed it to be the correct way to be. Indeed some teachers have difficulty relinquishing their role and need to remain in the master position. But if we take this equation to its logical conclusion, then we end up with subsequent generations of students with gradually diminishing levels of excellence. Instead, it's much wiser to continue to show respect to our teacher, while bringing about the full expression of our gift when we're practicing it. Only then can we be true to ourselves and of maximum benefit to those around us.

Now we get to the loyalty to our parents. We *need* them to be right, since not only are they in control of our health and wellbeing when we're small, but society reinforces the concept continuously through convention, religion and even culture. As a matter of fact, the French expression for "well behaved" translates literally to "well raised". The parents have the full responsibility to teach right and wrong, how to interact with others, and how to navigate everything from crossing the street safely to getting our first bank account.

It doesn't matter that not every parent is equipped for the job. Some really have no idea how to interact with little ones. Some are caught up in escape mechanisms to cope with their own issues, making it more difficult to be the parent they could be otherwise. Some are subconsciously falling into the patterns set by their own parents since they are the only models they know, making it more difficult to parent according to their own ideals. And some have so much difficulty loving themselves that as much as they love their children, they unwittingly pass on self-defeating beliefs and behaviors.

Spiked Brownies

A teen I'll call Rob was considered by his teachers to be rather brilliant. He was also a very talented gymnast and studied with a master to excel in acrobatics. Despite this promising beginning, Rob decided to bring drugs to a school event and was caught. He refused to recognize that what he had done was wrong and that his offense was worse than that of the other students who had partaken of his loot. He felt that he was a scapegoat because the consequences imposed by the school were more severe for him than for the others involved.

At the heart of Rob's behavior lay a need to be seen for more than his accomplishments. Since he did so well in school, no one ever expected that he had unmet emotional needs. He resented the fact that his needs weren't met, and at the same time, since those needs were highly discouraged in his family, he suppressed acknowledging those needs even to himself. His father actually blamed the school for the incident since they were the ones who had organized the event away from school grounds. Not only did Rob then take the lead from his father that he wasn't responsible, he also subconsciously needed to honor his father and emulate his beliefs. By aligning himself with his father, he was looking for the bond created by an "us against them" situation. The very lonely part of him deep down needed to be nurtured, and so he sought even higher achievements to obtain the needed approval. When he still didn't get what he wanted, some part of him rebelled, as demonstrated not only by his actions with the drugs, but also in the fact that he was involved in a serious car accident the week before and walked away unhurt. Consciously, he would never have admitted that he wanted the accident, but as the driver, his subconscious drove him to find a way, any way, to obtain the caring attention he so very much wanted. We all need to be vulnerable sometimes, and a reprieve from a continuous display of strength.

Rob demonstrated how we can be simultaneously resentful of our parents and ultimately loyal to them. We so desperately need to be validated by the ones who gave birth to us that we will do almost anything to please them. Honoring them and behaving like them is one way to do this, and a way to show them that we are just like them, so we really do belong in their tribe; they can be rightfully proud of us. Showing loyalty also means not offending their ego. So by never being more financially successful than them, by not achieving a higher level of education than they did, by having some of the same issues as them, we are aligning ourselves to them and showing them "proper respect". We may want to do things differently than them because we might have vowed never to be like them in some way, but this vow goes to war against our very deep loyalty to them. The feeling is very much like not wanting to repudiate our Creator. Literally.

If we use the word Creator to represent the deity of our religion, then it's a sin if we turn our back on that most powerful Presence. When we live our lives, we are still, to some degree, doing things in the hopes of garnering our parents' approval, even if they're no longer around. The same applies to the Creator. We live with the belief that the Creator will reward us with Heaven for following the edicts of our religion throughout our life, or we will be punished with a less favorable outcome otherwise. The Creator carries a corresponding role to that of our parents, is actually called the Father in some religions, so that we continuously strive to be good to "please" Him.

The Santa Claus story is another parallel, with the moniker of "Father Christmas" in some languages. If we are good as children we will get gifts under the tree on Christmas morning, or a lump of coal if we act poorly. He "knows" everything and can see us, even if we can't see him. He is the judge and the dispenser of the reward or punishment. All we can do is behave properly and hope that we get what we are asking for.

Yet another layer is our country. The word "patriotism" is derived from the Latin root "pater", which means father. If we set aside the memory of the Third Reich calling Germany the "Fatherland" during the Second World War, we are just as inclined to be loyal to our country as to our family and our Creator. We expect our country to protect us and to set the stage for us to prosper, and in return we grant it fierce loyalty, willing to die for what our country represents.

This is not a criticism of fables, patriotism or religion. As stated at the beginning of the book, the structure of laws at every level delivers an orderly society with accepted rules of engagement. It's been shown that having a well established Rule of Law is required for a society to make great progress and successfully invite business interactions with other countries.

Rather, the point here is more that we are deeply conditioned to hold some things as immutable, such as loyalty to our parents and other corresponding "fathers". As a result, we may have adopted some beliefs that were simply handed down to us as fact. When we look at our own choices now, it's important to differentiate between what we have inherited automatically as beliefs, and where we actually want to go. For example, there are groups of people who still outlaw homosexuality, even to the point of capital punishment. Using discernment means that we get to choose to respect each individual and their choices rather than jump to conclusions that others have made.

We can still honor our parents for bringing us into this world and doing the best they could. But we should not limit ourselves, our joys and our achievements out of a misplaced belief that we will somehow be disloyal to our parents if we are successful. Quite the opposite: regardless of our success, wouldn't we want the very best for our children? Wouldn't they honor us in the most wonderful way if they reached great happiness and heights in their careers? Let's consider *that* to be our display of loyalty and give ourselves the freedom to choose what we want our lives to contain.

Before we leave this topic, there is one more hidden reason why we might be limiting our success, albeit unconsciously. If we are unsuccessful, then we can point the finger to those who have hurt us when we were younger and show them we're still damaged. We may not want to let them off the hook. It's rather like banging your head against the wall hoping that the other person gets a headache, to paraphrase a saying. It's time to let that go. There is no need to self-sabotage anymore. We've gone through the process of forgiving them, of realizing that they acted out of their own confused thinking, and that it's time we moved on. It may have hurt, but we're ready to let it be part of the past and no longer part of the future. We get to choose now.

Sacrifice

The feeling of betrayal comes in many disguises. Consider our willingness to make a sacrifice, big or small, for a cause or an institution (from the family upwards). We may believe that by making the sacrifice, we will either be rewarded for our behavior, or at the very least we'll feel in very good standing in the situation.

But what if we later see evidence that our sacrifice either wasn't necessary, or didn't earn us the accolades we sought? An example is the case of Mary. A group of people were scheduled to board a bus and go on a day trip, including Mary, her daughter, and Mary's best friend and mentor, Sheila, who also happened to be the group organizer. When Mary's daughter still hadn't arrived by departure time, Sheila asked Mary to decide whether they should delay their departure and wait, or leave as scheduled. In Sheila's mind, she gave Mary full permission to make the decision. But in Mary's mind, she felt the pressure of making a decision that would please Sheila, and so they left without the daughter.

Many years later, when a similar situation arose but concerned Sheila's daughter, Sheila opted to wait. She considered the fact that this time was more of a family trip rather than a business trip, and she didn't see the contradiction that Mary perceived at once. When Mary later complained about the unfairness, Sheila couldn't understand how Mary could complain about a decision she had made herself so many years before.

In this case, Mary felt that making the sacrifice to leave her tardy daughter behind was repaid by the esteem she believed she received as a result of making the "right" decision, of operating by the rules. But in Mary's eyes, Sheila's decision years later made a mockery of her initial choice. She felt demoted to second tier, because her own daughter didn't seem to merit the favors accorded to Sheila's daughter. She also felt angry that in the end, she didn't really get rewarded for following the rules. She started to feel unsure of her standing around Sheila, and their relationship became somewhat strained. But when Mary reacted out of proportion with a totally innocent remark that Sheila's daughter made one day, Mary couldn't see how everything was connected to her feeling betrayed. She looked for explanations outside of herself, not realizing that she had projected her feelings of betrayal onto Sheila's daughter.

Similarly, there are stories of how people made huge sacrifices during times of war to support the war effort. So finding out that some companies emerged quite wealthy as a result of supplying goods to the war department wasn't welcomed news. Their own sacrifices felt devalued, and their ego a little offended in the process.

Yet another example concerns those of us who gave up the life we knew in order to pursue our spiritual path. Many of us lost friends in the process because our old friends didn't know what to make of the "new" us. We disconnected from world news because they're too depressing. We became voracious readers of all things related to our spiritual path and attended conferences aimed at personal development and enlightenment. This made us wiser and more loving, and to a large degree, helped us make sense of our existence.

But what it didn't do was provide us with financial independence. Many of us went into service to humanity in various forms. We fell into the Priest archetype, where service to humanity is done for free from our hearts, and money is expected to be contributed towards our support somehow.

We sacrificed much along this journey, including the perceived safety net of a set of rules that we were familiar with. When we begin the journey, at first we feel alone, that there's no one to talk to about our growing yearnings. Then we may choose one path that a particular teacher is on and follow it, or realize that none of the practices adopted by others exactly fits us, so we need to forge ahead with no roadmap. There may have been years when we wandered without a clear understanding of where this unrelenting yearning wanted to lead us. And most of us felt we had a mission we were meant to achieve, but that we couldn't quite identify it.

The sacrifices felt at times overwhelming, but we were so sure that our path would lead us exactly where we were meant to be that we persisted. Little did we realize that, for the vast majority of us, we still need to recognize that we are responsible for tending to our human reality. This includes taking care of our bodies, our relationships and our finances. We need to return to this planet, as the song *Drops of Jupiter* so aptly describes. We need to engage in our everyday world in a way that combines our higher ideals and our spiritual awareness, with a full embodiment of our physical selves, right down to our toes. We need to stop dreaming that a miracle will appear in the form of a lottery or other windfall, and find ways to interact with a world that is not yet perfect. We may like to remain in a blissful state and not have to deal with the dirty details of everyday life, but, sorry, the dishes still have to be done.

This can come as a bit of a crushing blow to many of us. We made the sacrifice, the lived years of the spiritual life, and we believe Heaven should be at the other end of this journey. We don't realize that *we* are the ones to create this Heaven. *We* are the ones to bring back what we learned from Jupiter and incorporate it so seamlessly into our everyday lives that we improve our own direct environment, and affect everyone we touch as a result. *We* are the ones responsible for taking those actions that lead to a better tomorrow. We can have a huge impact merely by projecting positive energy from a place of pure thought, but we will have a much bigger impact by intermingling with all of humanity and finding creative solutions to current world hiccups.

Life doesn't seem to be playing by the rules we had envisioned. We can resist the truth that is facing us and encounter ongoing hardships, or we can choose to move forward, given what we have. If we feel disappointed, let's acknowledge that, release the feeling of implied betrayal, and choose a new perspective for tomorrow.

Let's start fresh. We have new insights and the reward for our journey has been all of the ways we have grown. Let's make that a pillar of our strength, and take the reins of our lives back. We worked hard. We deserve to be there for ourselves.

6 NOT GUILTY!

Have you ever had the experience where you thought about someone and shortly thereafter, they called, texted or emailed you? How can that possibly happen? Coincidence?

Nope! What is actually taking place is that our thoughts produce little electrical waves, as measured by medical instruments. It's exactly like placing a cell phone call, but the hardware is inside our heads. Those little waves traveled to the person we were "dialing", and that person's internal cell phone receiver picked up on the call. They didn't realize this was happening, of course, but for some reason, they just started thinking about us! So they reached out can contacted us through more regular channels.

Consider that this happens every time you think about someone. Not only that, but these internal cell phones have an extra built-in feature. Not only can they send and receive calls, they also send and receive the emotion that was expressed when the call was made. Just like with regular phones, our recipient can hear if we're expressing joy or love, and they also hear if we're angry at them, blaming them or any other negative feeling.

Oops.

Before you totally freak out, remember. You didn't know. You were just having a party in the privacy of your own head. But now that you do know, doesn't that give the recommendation to manage your thoughts a whole new meaning?

OK, so we need to take responsibility here. And this includes understanding just what happens when we feel guilty about something.

We are raised to believe that it's honorable to feel guilty if we did something to someone that is judged wrong. After all, that shows we're penitent, and that's part of the punishment that leads to restitution in our Creator's eyes, for example. Some people actually take advantage of the fact that feeling penitent makes us vulnerable to manipulation and they get people to do things for them by pressing on their guilt button.

The other belief is that by feeling guilty, it'll ensure that we won't do it again. This is all well and good, but feeling guilty actually causes far more harm than you think. And not just for us.

Feeling guilty eats away at us. It convinces us that we are "bad". It prevents us from being our entire self. It sets up a cycle of self-punishment. It interferes with our relationships because we may try to make up for the fact that we feel guilty and behave unnaturally as a consequence.

One woman I'll call Judy was the driver in a serious car accident. She recognized she was at fault, and she suffered long-term physical trauma. But much worse is that she lost her young daughter in the accident. Judy refused to let go of her guilt and was almost constantly depressed. She was afraid, five years later, that if she stopped feeling guilty, she would somehow start to forget about her daughter. If she couldn't move forward, then at least she was still back in that place where she felt full of her daughter, even if it meant pain. When Judy understood that she would always remember her little girl, and that her daughter would much prefer that Judy find happiness again, Judy relented and released the guilt. She went on to compete in triathlons afterwards, an incredible feat for someone who had been in pain merely going up the stairs.

The second person being harmed by our guilt is *the person we're feeling guilty about in the first place.* When we feel guilty, the thought behind the emotion is "I've harmed you. I've harmed you. I've harmed you." Feeling guilty is actually a self-running program in the background, never very far from the surface.

Now, remember the internal cell phone we all have. That means the other person keeps hearing, at a subconscious level, "I've been harmed. I've been harmed. I've been harmed." If their subconscious believes they've been harmed, then they act harmed. And their lives don't work so well.

On the other hand, when we release the guilt, we relieve the other person from that negative tape. The result is a much better experience for both. This doesn't give us permission to act without considering consequences. It just means that something took place in the past, we own it, we apologize, we decide that it's not the kind of thing we want to do again because it didn't feel good for anybody, and we move on with life, free of the burden of the self-imposed prison. It also releases the other person from the burden of remaining a victim. *Even if we never actually talk to them about it.*

I've seen miracles take place as a result of the following exercise.

Find a very comfortable chair, or lie down. Close your eyes. Take three very slow breaths, and with each exhale, feel yourself relax. Think of the other person who is the source of your guilty feelings. Let's call this person Joe for this exercise, but please substitute the person's actual name. Imagine Joe is at a point into the distance. Invite Joe to meet you, somewhere in the middle. This way, Joe gets to come of his own accord and on his own timing. When Joe appears, go to him, and tell him how very sorry you are. Tell him that you love him, and you want only good things for him. Offer him a hug, and as you embrace, just keep repeating to him, from your heart, "I love you", while you are smiling broadly, happy to be reunited. You will feel the emotion that was there before completely melt away, and Joe will leave when he is ready. Realize that you have just changed two lives, and touched, as a ripple effect, the lives of all the people around you both.

The Other Direction

This same concept works in the reverse direction as well. If someone is feeling guilty about something they did to us, we are living under a constant rainfall of "I've been harmed". If you've ever given yourself a complete beautiful clearing, as described in Chapter 2 for example, then you feel simply wonderful. But then the next day things don't feel quite so wonderful anymore. Though there could be a very wide variety of reasons for this, one may be that someone is feeling guilty about you and you're picking up on it. The clearing disconnected you from that energy link, but the other person was still linking to you through their guilt, and you started feeling it again.

It's like living in a city with very high air pollution. You might be able to get pure oxygen from a tank and completely clear your lungs, but the pollution is still there and eventually you'll be breathing it in again.

So repeat the same exercise as above, but switch the roles. First, make a list of everyone you believe may be feeling guilty about anything they did back to day one. Leave out the small details, but guilt is a feeling that can live a long time, so don't discount who it is that comes to mind.

Then, one by one, invite these individuals to meet you in this sacred place that you create in your mind. Notice their look of contrition and explain to them that you have completely forgiven them. Offer them a big hug and give them all the love you have in your heart. This will completely transform them, and release you from the negative bond that was keeping the two of you connected in this unproductive cycle. When you've completed the process with that person, you can invite the next person to join you.

This actually doesn't take very long to do, but it's very powerful and can have a significant impact on you.

I'm Next!

You had to know this was coming. Now we get to the very crux of the matter.

We must release any feelings of guilt that we hold towards ourselves. But before we get to the actual process, let's look at how we got there in the first place.

We need to feel safe.

==> Being loved means that we will be taken care of so we need to feel loved.

==> We don't feel as loved as we need, so we try to be and do better to get the love.

==> We are taught about right and wrong. We learn that we get rewarded for right and punished for wrong.

==> Since we're not getting that love we want, then we must have been or done wrong somehow.

==> We try to be and do right, but it's still not giving us the results we want.

==> So we must really be wrong then. Especially since we have feelings that are judged wrong, such as anger and jealousy.

==> Wow, we're really wrong. So we deserve to be punished.

==> We punish ourselves by berating ourselves on a regular basis. That's the right thing to do because that's what you're supposed to get if you're wrong.

==> The only way we're ever going to feel right is if we become perfect. Only then can we get the reward, because then we'll be right.

==> We push ourselves to achieve, because that seems to represent right. But achievements feel good for such a short amount of time. Achievements didn't erase all the other aspects of us that are still wrong.

==> So we must try harder, achieve more, and never give ourselves a break because we need to be punished for as long as we're still wrong.

==> So when a reward does come, we're not really allowed to enjoy it because, since we're still wrong, we don't really deserve the reward.

==> We feel guilty about being wrong because that's not how you're supposed to be and it must be our fault. We feel guilty every time we do something wrong because it doesn't honor those who taught us, those who believe in us, and those who rely on us. We feel guilty every time we do something that feels like a reward, like eating cake, because not only do we not deserve the reward yet, the reward itself takes us further away from fixing what is wrong with us, in this case our health or weight. We feel guilty about charging what we think we're worth, because it implies bragging and placing ourselves first, two behaviors that are considered wrong. And we feel guilty charging for something that we find easy and fun to do, because work is supposed to be hard to deserve a financial reward.

Before we beat ourselves up for beating ourselves up, let's consider that this entire sequence happens below the radar of our conscious mind, and it's actually something that happens to almost every one of us. This deserves some tapping to reduce the welling up of emotion that just got stirred up.

Karate chop point: 1. Even though I've been so hard on myself for so long, I deeply and completely see that I did this without meaning to harm myself.
2. Even though it's been so long since I really allowed myself to enjoy a reward, I deeply and completely commit to changing that now.
3. Even though I have so much catching up to do in terms of loving myself, I deeply and completely accept that today is the perfect day to start.

Eyebrow: I was so hard on myself
Side of the eye: I thought I deserved it
Under the eye: I really believed there was something wrong with me
Under the nose: And that wrong needed to be punished
Chin: But now I'm willing to see

Collar bone: That the definition of wrong was all wrong!
Under the arm: That there was no benefit to beating myself up

Top of the head: Because I thought I wasn't good enough

Eyebrow: I am so ready to let this go
Side of the eye: This being hard on myself
Under the eye: This judging myself
Under the nose: This believing that I'm not good enough
Chin: I am so ready to let that go!
Collar bone: There's nothing to be gained
Under the arm: From thinking I need to be fixed
Top of the head: Instead, I'm going to do it differently now

Eyebrow: I'm going to choose to honor myself
Side of the eye: To honor that everything I've been through
Under the eye: Everything I've put myself through
Under the nose: Has just been in preparation
Chin: For accepting myself completely now
Collar bone: For understanding that there was never anything wrong in the first place
Under the arm: That I just misunderstood the situation
Top of the head: And now I see reality in a completely new light

Eyebrow: Right and wrong are not so rigid after all
Side of the eye: What's right to one person looks wrong to another
Under the eye: So it's up to me to decide

Under the nose: To look deep inside and choose for myself
Chin: What I want to believe
Collar bone: How I want to see the world
Under the arm: And I'm going to see it with way more latitude
Top of the head: Than I ever thought was possible before

Eyebrow: I'm going to give myself the love I've always wanted
Side of the eye: I'm going to drop this concept of reward and punishment
Under the eye: I'm just going to do what I can and experience life
Under the nose: Find out what I like and what I don't
Chin: And never see things from a reward and punishment point of view
Collar bone: Just see the results of what I do to be simply results
Under the arm: And adjust course if I'd rather have different results
Top of the head: That feels so much better

Eyebrow: I'm so excited to have this new lease on life
Side of the eye: It feels completely different now
Under the eye: It's going to be so much more fun
Under the nose: I get to enjoy what I do
Chin: I get to give myself permission to try new things
Collar bone: And if they don't turn out how I'd like
Under the arm: Then I'll just try something else
Top of the head: Because my life is there for me to live!

Take a deep breath.

7 HIDE AND GO SEEK

When we think that we are wrong somehow, we believe exposing those wrongs will push people away, resulting in even less love coming our way. So we need to hide those wrongs, and the easiest way to do that is by hiding altogether.

The place that comes to mind immediately when we want to hide is home. Home is supposed to be our sanctuary, where we can really be ourselves and relax. Home is where no one can reach us unless we invite them in. And as adults, home can be according to our own design, living alone if that's what we wish.

But for some crazy reason, home doesn't deliver on those promises. Home carries many responsibilities, and when we are there, we see the housework, the yardwork, the cooking, the repairs, all of those tasks that we should be doing. This is why most people find a vacation away from home more relaxing than a "staycation". Home represents the "everyday", rather than the special and extraordinary adventures we can experience when we're away. But the real reason lies below the surface.

Our home of origin was where rules were laid down first. Rules restricted who and how we were allowed to be. Home was where the routines were and routines started feeling like more rules. Home basically told us that until we obeyed all the rules faithfully, we didn't deserve freedom yet, because we couldn't even behave when we were under the watchful guidance of the rule keepers.

So home felt restrictive. It was where we first "learned" that we were not OK, that we were wrong. It was where we were grounded when we didn't follow the rules. It was where we first felt bullied, or abandoned, or that we didn't belong. And we couldn't really complain, couldn't actually run away, because we had nowhere else to go. We were stuck.

We project those past associations onto the place we now call home. Home can come to feel somewhat like a prison. It places demands on us. Home still carries all the rules and judgment in our subconscious mind. So even home doesn't let us hide when we want to. Which can send us in search of distractions, such as TV or overwork, or an addiction, all of which deliver feel-good chemicals in the brain and allow us to escape for a while.

We need to make home a safe haven again. We could tap, but let's address this differently.

Close your eyes. Imagine placing a huge suitcase on top of your bed. In this suitcase, put all the rules, the ways you felt wrong, the hurtful things that you heard, the feeling that you were stuck, everything that you associated with your home growing up that didn't feel good. Pluck all of those items from all around the house, even from the walls and ceilings. Place the suitcase outside your front door, and see a delivery truck come pick up your baggage. Now picture the outside of your house, and place a large tinsel star over the house, in the middle of the roof line. The house is now like a Christmas tree, a place to celebrate, a place to connect with loved ones, and a place where we can have fun and joy, every day of the year. Now see the tinsel snow down all over the house from the central star, and see it flow through every space in the house, every room, hallway, closet, every single nook and cranny. All the way to the foundation, where it accumulates into a shiny floor. Next, imagine a long garland of lovely tiny white lights wrapped all around the inside of every room. The whole house has been infused with the energy of celebration and joy. Finally, see a beautiful jewelry box appear on your bedroom dresser. It contains the most valuable of all jewels, love. When you lift the lid, you can feel the love washing through you and filling the whole room. You can lift this lid for as long as you wish, anytime it pleases you. This is your home now. This is your home.

As you open your eyes, you may feel the difference in how you perceive the house. It will allow you to hide if you want, but it's actually giving you what you seek, which is acceptance. We love you, say all the rooms in your home. Welcome home.

8 THE SUB

If we've felt that we didn't get what we needed from our parents, then we'll look for someone else as a substitute. For example, if we felt abandoned by our mother, we may subconsciously be trying to find the validation and nurturing we needed through another woman. She may be a teacher, a mentor, an older female friend, or we may even fall in love with a woman who, in our eyes, will supply us with the complete acceptance and support that we believe a mother should grant us.

The same goes if we didn't have a strong, supportive, and protective male role model. Substitute father figures include a coach, a romantic partner who will provide for us and make us feel safe, a business mentor who takes us under his wing, a country, or a deity. Most religions, save a few that are less mainstream such as Wicca, have a male figure as the Father, the Creator, the Omnipotent and Omniscient One.

We may find ourselves believing that if we serve (our country, our spirituality), our needs will be met somehow. If we sacrifice and put others before us, we will be redeemed - anything we may have done or even thought in the past will be forgiven as we have achieved the true spiritual self.

We give at least some of our power away to those people or beliefs we seek to satisfy our need for love and safety. But any parental substitute, be it a new relationship or an institution, will come with its own set of rules and expectations. In our ideal view, we would receive what we need, finally feel really good about ourselves, and this would allow us to embark on the career or any other venture that requires courage and confidence.

The parental role consists of creating a strong foundation from which we can launch. Once we feel we have the foundation, then we want to spring forth and declare our independence. We demonstrate this as young adults by leaving the parental home, but as full adults, the urge to express our independence can cause us to want to change our circumstances. We appreciate what we received, but we want to gain freedom from the rules set by someone else, even if those rules are simply implied, as can be the case in a romantic relationship. We want to distance ourselves from the environment we were in when we were still in the "before" stage. We want our surroundings to reflect the new us, and that impulse can leave collateral damage.

A variation of this scenario occurs when we meet someone who appears to have the potential to satisfy our needs. We project onto that person, and relationship if applicable, qualities that are amplified with our hope of having found a solution to our problem. When the person starts to meet our needs, the needs become less urgent, and they exert less influence over our perception of reality. Then we may come to realize that the person/relationship is not as good a fit as we once genuinely believed. We start moving away emotionally, and possibly physically, from the situation. We are being true to ourselves, but at the same time, we realize that we had given the other person hopes and expectations that were based on our initially skewed perception. The other person may not even have done anything wrong; all they did was be themselves and validate us in the process. We had thought that validation would bring us salvation, when in fact, all it did was show us that the validation didn't really serve us the way we had expected it would. The other person ends up hurt and confused. Though we were acting out of genuine feeling initially, it may turn out differently than we first imagined.

If we were on the other side of this, we could feel betrayed. One woman I'll call Liz spoke sadly about her broken marriage. She said her husband had promised to love her forever, to never leave her. Then she frowned fiercely and exclaimed "He lied!" She had given her power to the illusion that the relationship would make her feel safe forever. When the illusion was dispelled, the shock to her sense of wholeness stunned her. She repainted her past with a new belief that she had been misled, and all those happy memories no longer shone as brightly.

When we lose an illusion that we created, especially if it's connected to a spouse or a best friend, the pain can be quite intense. If we need an illusion to hold up, we are quite good at disregarding any evidence to the contrary. But not only do we lose what we thought was a strong connection, we may also start wondering how we'll be able to find an honest relationship. We were so sure, and we turned out to be wrong. If we can't really connect to others, we may end up alone, without a tribe, and a low-grade panic can set in. The need for the tribe is ancient, and not necessarily conscious.

By recognizing that emotions can change over time, move from passion to companionship or something else, and at each moment still be true, we can make more peace with reality. We can find a way to be grateful for the beautiful moments we did have, and allow ourselves to move on. We may mourn the lost closeness and the hope our illusion brought us, but it's better to acknowledge what is the actual situation and make choices based on that. If we can find the way to retain our own power, and not give it to an illusion, then we are much better off in the first place.

Let's do a tapping round to hit the energy of betrayal squarely between the eyes. And we'll do the setup phrase afterwards because it fits better there in this case.

Eyebrow: You betrayed me!
Side of the eye: You lied to me!
Under the eye: I was so good to you and this is how you thank me?
Under the nose: How could you do this to me?
Chin: You promised!
Collar bone: You said we were family
Under the arm: That we would be together forever
Top of the head: But you broke your promise

Eyebrow: You betrayed me
Side of the eye: And it really hurt
Under the eye: I thought we were so close

Under the nose: And you turn around and do this
Chin: I can't believe I put my trust in you
Collar bone: After all I've done for you
Under the arm: This is how you treat me
Top of the head: I didn't deserve this

Eyebrow: You betrayed me
Side of the eye: And I'm not sure I can forgive that
Under the eye: I really needed you
Under the nose: And now I've lost that
Chin: And I'm left with nothing
Collar bone: You broke a trust
Under the arm: You betrayed me
Top of the head: And I'm really angry about that

Eyebrow: But now I can see
Side of the eye: You probably didn't do it on purpose
Under the eye: I was needy
Under the nose: And you filled my need
Chin: I'm really sorry to lose that
Collar bone: To lose you whom I love
Under the arm: But now it's time to let go
Top of the head: Let you live your life and me live mine

Eyebrow: You hurt me
Side of the eye: But you're not really to blame
Under the eye: You did your best in the end
Under the nose: It just didn't work out how I hoped
Chin: And I can't really blame you for that
Collar bone: I projected too much onto you
Under the arm: Onto our relationship
Top of the head: And now it's time to let that go.

Karate chop point: 1. Even though I was so angry, I deeply and completely allow myself to release that feeling. 2. Even though I blamed you for it, I deeply and completely recognize that we had a beautiful story, and now it's time for the next one. 3. Even though there's so much that I had hoped for, I deeply and completely accept that there's much to love in my future.

Take a deep breath.

9 THE BODYGUARDS

As described earlier, our most powerful instinct is for survival and this instinct is primal. We also saw how this instinct can be triggered by feeling that we are not secure in our relationships and environment, even if our insecurities are strictly at the emotional level.

There are two main immediate ways that I've seen people react when they feel their sense of safety threatened and I'll call them the Bodyguards. The first Bodyguard goes on the attack from a fierce need to defend the Self. It generates an angry retort, or can even go into rage if what was triggered is a particularly sensitive point. The second Bodyguard adopts the reverse stance. He throws himself around us, completely shielding us from the possible harm of the situation. These are the two facets of the fight or flight response. And we can find ourselves inviting both at different times.

Bodyguard Number One

These two Bodyguards are just trying to protect us. But the first one is not well received in society. Anger and rage disrupt smooth communications. Their expression is not respected because they are perceived as a loss of self-control. When we behave that way in response to a trigger, it's actually true that we lose control. The outburst feels involuntary, even if it's kept to ourselves and we steam on the inside. We are likely to blame the other person for "making" us angry or fearful.

But because anger is so criticized, we will tend to swallow it and try to pretend that it's not there, even to ourselves. That can lead to serious health effects, because the anger didn't actually disappear. It only vanished from our awareness. If we don't deal with our emotions, they accumulate in the body and create problems in the same way as consuming heavy metals (such as mercury) accumulate silently in the body until the body can no longer tolerate its toxic environment. We then experience symptoms of disease without understanding their cause. Symptoms of anger can include heartburn, ulcers, high blood pressure, colon issues (which, in turn, can lead to low absorption of nutrients, leading to a whole host of other issues), and headaches.

So if expressing anger is not considered acceptable, and repressing it is also a problem, then how do we deal with anger? It's up to us to understand what triggered us to anger and to dissolve it. This is best done with someone who will support us but is not the cause or target of our anger. Some of us have gone this route often enough that we can do it in the privacy of our own minds, but for most of us, getting a trusted and impartial viewpoint can help. What is needed here is not someone who will agree with us that it's all the other person's fault! What we really need is to keep turning it back onto our own selves. This is about us. Not about the other, however much it feels that way, regardless of the inappropriateness of their action. Obviously, I'm not advocating excusing behavior in someone that can put us in danger. But for the most part, the emotional wounds are our own, and it's up to us to heal them.

Some helpful questions to ask ourselves about the situation:

- What was it specifically that the other person did or said that set me off?

- What about that trigger makes me angry in particular?

- What does what happened say about me? For example, if they implied that I didn't fulfill a duty, then that might mean (to me) that they don't think I'm suitable for the role and they'll look for someone else instead, which threatens my sense of security and my ego.

- When is the first time something like this happened (that specific trigger)? This could be in childhood and look different than today's events, but it still fired up a connection to the original occurrence.

- How can I look at that first occurrence with adult eyes instead of the eyes of a wholly-dependent child? How can I reassure the child that still lives in me that what happened in the past felt threatening, but in actual fact, things would turn out OK and we would survive the incident, physically and emotionally?

- If today's event had happened to someone else who didn't have that original childhood event, would they have reacted in the same way?

- How would I prefer to interpret this exact scenario if/when it happens again? Can I insert a little "pattern interrupt pause" before the anger sets in to reassure myself that I'll be OK?

- What are the words that I really want to hear to reassure me in this situation? Can I tell myself these same words and believe them?

Our Bodyguard lives inside us. He comes out when he believes we need him. So if we feel him raising his head attentively, we can place our hands on our lower abdomens and repeat to ourselves, "It's OK. I'm safe. I can handle this. You can go back to sleep. I know you're there and I'll call you if I need you." This will greatly help to maintain our calm and choose our response in the present, rather than reacting based on hurts from the past.

Bodyguard Number Two

The other Bodyguard comes in when we feel that expressing anger is dangerous. If we fear that someone will leave us if we become angry, then we might bypass the anger altogether and go into a protective shell, compliments of the second Bodyguard. In this way, we are taking a step back from the situation, not feeling it entirely, because it's too painful. This sounds like a viable solution, and our Bodyguard is only too happy to oblige.

But in creating that protective shield, we are suppressing our ability to truly feel the joys that life has to offer. And there is a second, more insidious side effect. By adopting this coping mechanism, we are effectively telling our body that the world is not safe, which is why we need this protective covering. Our body can then create concrete evidence of our belief and start reacting negatively to what should be fairly harmless substances. Severe allergies can be the result. After all, it is the immune system's job to react against what it considers to be foreign intruders that could harm us. And if we feel deeply unsafe in the world, then the immune system can go into complete overdrive, blindly attacking everything, including our body's own tissues. Thus an autoimmune disease may emerge. This is not to say that all autoimmune diseases begin this way. But it's one of the possible causes. If we react strongly to substances such as perfume, this gives us the perfect opportunity to stay home, thereby keeping us away from possible "dangers".

Another way our body could respond is with fatigue. When the second Bodyguard shows up, we retreat into the perceived safety of his shield. But what is actually going on is that we are choosing to reduce ourselves as a result of an external threat to our emotional safety. Even if it's only symbolic, a self-protective stance is by definition curved in on itself, which impedes deep breathing. Without proper oxygen delivered to the cells, we can't produce energy very well.

The other aspect of this Bodyguard is that it will take a permanent presence in our lives if we are constantly feeling unsafe at the subconscious level. This sets us up for chronic vigilance, always on alert for possible threats. Chronic vigilance results in constant demands on the adrenal glands to produce coritsol and adrenaline, hormones that are meant to surge during times of danger and excitement. As a chronic condition, however, this results in adrenal fatigue, which makes it nearly impossible for the body to produce sufficient energy. Add to that how cortisol interferes with sleep, and not only does the body have difficulty producing energy, but it also can't recover properly during its critical nightly ritual.

The symbolic representation that is happening in the body is that if we feel we constantly need protection, then at some level we feel like a victim. Our protection mechanisms themselves reduce our ability to choose from a broad range of options offered by Life, limiting us to a few safe, proven choices. To a large degree, this takes much of the spark out of life, as we are meant to be creative, expansive beings. A car whose spark plugs have become old and worn, will see its mileage deteriorate greatly. In other words, the engine is receiving the same fuel as before, but it's not turning that fuel into energy for the car to use to move forward very well.

Our bodies are acting the same way, both physically and emotionally. We need to feel safe enough to venture out beyond the limitations of our Bodyguards, and recognize that we have more choice than we realized.

Or...

Our real strength doesn't come from Bodyguard Number One. Fighting back can look like a show of strength, but in fact, it's merely a tactic in a fight, as in "the best defense is a good offense". Maybe the better strategy is to not engage in the fight in the first place. This doesn't mean avoiding all circumstances that can lead to conflict. It means seeing any situation as an opportunity to understand that the other person may be showing us their Bodyguards at the moment rather than their true selves.

Instead of relying on Bodyguards, however, it's in our *vulnerability* that we can find our greatest strength. We've been led to believe that being vulnerable is the same as being weak, but it's only because we haven't known the potential that this very special part of us carries.

None of us really knows what tomorrow holds. We might have made plans and think we're in control, but in fact, anything can happen on the way to the meeting. If we can recognize this, and still trust that we will be able to deal with whatever comes up, that somehow Life will provide us with opportunities to find a solution, then we are giving our vulnerable side an equal voice to that of our ego. The ego may run the show most of the time, sure of its individuality. But when we are faced with the unpredictable, the ego doesn't know what to do anymore.

On the other hand, if we allow our vulnerability to express its real strength, then it will stand tall and allow us to receive what it is that we need to decide how to proceed with the situation at hand, regardless of where the assistance comes from. It may be an inspiration, a helping hand, or an incredible coincidence. By being open to these, we will be more likely to see them, recognize them as such, and receive them in a way that will be helpful for all.

In a crisis, the ego may want to go into survival mode. The vulnerable self can stay calm and operate from its ability to be completely present to the moment. It demonstrates to us how to receive graciously, with no inclination to feel guilty about it.

By giving our vulnerable self permission to emerge and engage with us, we are more able to trust that we do have the strength, we do have the power, we do have the ability to choose. By letting our Bodyguards know that we are feeling safer, we open ourselves up to receiving what we have been wanting all along, to really partake of the joys of being alive right now.

10 THE BODY

Why our body does what it does is sometimes a mystery to us. If it gets sick, breaks out in fat at the mere sight of cake, or produce grey hairs before we're ready for them, we might feel betrayed by it.

The key here is to remember that everything that we feel or fear shows up in the body. It is often the most accurate mirror of what's going on in our heads, which includes the subconscious mind.

The subconscious mind likes to run the show. It wants to tell us what to avoid to keep us safe. It'll try to prevent us from doing something new out of the fear that anything new, by definition, potentially carries unknown outcomes. The known is safe ground, even if it's not really what we want. Public speaking makes us feel very vulnerable in front of many people, so the subconscious creates a great fear to keep us away from this danger zone.

If there's something we really don't want to do, the subconscious mind is clever enough to manufacture an illness or an accident to prevent us from having to go through the unwanted experience. Similarly, if we really need to be nurtured, as mentioned before, we may find ourselves in a situation where we have no choice in the matter (again, such as an illness or accident). It's too difficult for the ego to express the need for nurturing, so it gives the job to the subconscious mind, which delivers!

If we're afraid of moving forward in some way, such as starting a new business, the body might become blocked somewhere. It could be in the circulatory system (blood clot), the nervous system (pinched nerve), or the skeletal structure (locked up joint).

The body is *very* literal. Betrayal feels like being "stabbed in the back", meaning back spasms or intense back pain. Betrayal can also feel like a "slap in the face", lighting up jaw issues. Betrayal has also been known to "suck the air out of us", leading to asthma, or feeling weak and fatigued, with little energy to work on our projects.

Inflammation can come from anger or tension. Being "brought down to our knees" can transform into knee and quadriceps issues. Feeling very sad, we can be "choked up" and develop throat problems. If an event has taken us completely by surprise, we might be "struck dumb", and suddenly have trouble remembering words.

Our bodies are not betraying us. Quite the contrary, they're trying to protect us, and alert us as to what's going on in the mind. It's the same function as pain. Pain serves to point out that there is an injury somewhere, and we need to tend to that area and protect it until it's healed. Think of your body symptoms in the same way.

I've seen someone have kidney stones from being unable to express emotions. The kidney is a filter, and the emotions accumulated there. Someone else developed a large lump on the side of his neck to "protect his jugular" against someone he believed would lash out at him. Sounds very strange, but it really does work this way.

Our primary task, then, is to not get angry at the body. Instead, let's make a point of listening to it and understand the message that it's trying to convey. It's like a puzzle to solve. It's tempting to get angry at the puzzle if we haven't found the answer yet, but it really doesn't do any good. Let's give our body the love it wants, in return for all the work it does 24 hours a day for us.

The other part of our body that sometimes feels like a miscreant is our mind. We might forget things when we need to remember them, have mood swings, find it difficult to focus, or have trouble falling asleep because of "monkey mind".

Here's the good news. Despite all that the subconscious mind does in order to serve us, despite the fact that we had adopted an inner bully and placed it directly at the forefront of our thoughts, despite the bewildering array of things our mind does that we're not happy with, like driving us to eat those chips, the bottom line is…

… We have complete control over our minds.

We just have to choose that to be the case. By the sheer fact that I've written three books on how to clear the past from our minds and cells, it's obvious that I don't think it's entirely that simple. But we've done the work now. We've cleared so many things from our past that further digging is just going to produce more stuff to clear. There's a point at which we have to declare that it's enough. We'll deal with what comes in the future, and we have a list of tools to help us do that. We've made such amazing progress, we've healed our past to such a degree, we have come to understand so well why we behave the way we do, that we've come to a place where we can turn the page and declare that we are the ones choosing what goes on in there now.

As I write, today is July 4th. That means Independence Day here in the United States. It's a perfect day to declare our freedom from events and beliefs from the past. Any day is the right day to start the rest of our lives, as cliché as that sounds. But today, we draw a line in the sand. Today we turn the page to a future where we get to choose with the information in the present, not from fears born in the past. Today is a day, not only of hope, but of knowing that we have the power to take control of how we feel, because we are the only ones who can choose that.

Regardless of what happens around us, or how other people choose to behave, we have come to this place where we can finally start living. We leave our baggage at the curb, and we don't run back to retrieve it. We have made a decision, and we can already feel any remaining weight from the past fade away. We are lighter, we are sunnier, and we have decided what's really important for us.

If we brought someone a beautiful potted plant, and our friend cut off the flowers to put them in a vase, and then threw away the rest of the plant, we would be dismayed at the waste. Every day that the plant lives, it brings us joy, not only when it blooms. Let your life be like that. Every day that we live brings us experiences. Let's celebrate those experiences of life, the process of discovery, the development phase of a project, the time spent with others. We celebrate awards and weddings, but real happiness comes from delighting in all the events in between.

Let's choose to have a good life, by finding and bringing joy every day. Let's close this chapter of our lives by knowing that we decide if something is difficult or a challenge. We decide how completely we'll open our hearts and give of ourselves in that next hug.

If thoughts were people, we would be much choosier whom we allow in our heads. Let's decide to invite the friendly ones to live with us, and ask the others to decamp. Let's structure our minds to be the most nurturing home for us. A place that is safe, a place that is welcoming, a place where being ourselves is the happiest of options.

Let's give ourselves the love we've always wanted. Let's recognize that we are the person we've been looking for all along. Let's give Life gratitude for trying to show this to us all along.

Let's not waste another minute.
Choose wonder. Choose joy. Choose love.
Choose you.

11 ONE MORE TIME!

I was so hoping that the last chapter ended the book. Did you ever see the movie *"Best Friends"*, with Goldie Hawn and Burt Reynolds? At one point, they're in a small room, discussing a serious topic. Then Burt's character makes this great pronouncement, and walks out. Except that the door is locked and he can't leave. They turn the serious moment into a failed grand exit and the tension eases with a chuckle.

Well, this is exactly what just happened. I thought I had wrapped up the topic, subject to a few revisions. But then Life intervened to give me what may be the greatest "a-ha" of all about betrayal through two almost-three-year-old boys who don't know each other. As usual, I'm making up the names for them.

The first one is Aaron, a darling little boy who follows requests from his parents immediately, and who is growing into a healthy child. His mother's concern, however, is that he doesn't speak yet. He resists all attempts at being directed to speak by adults, but has been heard to repeat things like "helicopter" if his siblings said it. So there is no physical constraint, just an emotional one. Aaron has been fearful of adults ever since he had a seizure at 16 months and was poked and prodded in the hospital, where they attempted to understand what happened.

The second boy is Jason. He was badly mistreated in his first 14 months, completely neglected by his parents and passed on to any adult who would be willing to look after him for a while, including people who weren't equipped to do so. When he was taken away from his parents by Child Services, a distant relative adopted him and helped to restore his life, giving him a stable home. He was able to recuperate from all the illnesses that he had accumulated and is thriving in his new family. But recently, the new parents bought Jason a puppy to give him a playmate, since his adoptive siblings are all quite a bit older than him. To the parents' distress, Jason showed a new side of his personality and made a point of abusing the puppy when he came near it, something he never did with other people's pets.

What's going on in Jason's personality is an exaggeration of what many of us are feeling. For the first several years of our lives, we are completely dependent on the older members of our family for survival. This extends to parents as well as older siblings, and any other adult authority figure in our lives. We recognize that we need the older people, and we are on the receiving end of their generosity.

If we are mistreated or neglected by them, we don't allow ourselves to complain about that because they're all we have. But we come to see that the older ones are not protecting us in the way that they should. They have power over us and are not honoring the responsibility that comes with that power.

In Jason's case, at the first opportunity of his having power over another, his deep-set anger at having been mistreated by others who had power over him emerged. He felt compelled to hand down the same treatment that he received. He needed revenge somehow, and the poor puppy, who had done nothing to deserve it, was on the receiving end. The puppy was the only one whose love Jason didn't depend on.

Dishing out the anger didn't help though. It would keep coming back until he clears it, and the only way to do that is energetically. At under 3, he's too young to comprehend what's going on inside him that makes him behave this way. His former abuse made such an impact on him that part of him wants to hang onto that anger and mete it out when the opportunity presents itself. Anger energizes us. His tiger bodyguard was huge, and when it was acknowledged and seen by me, it was willing to walk away. Jason needs a little time to recover from this major shift within himself, but he'll be OK.

We see similar behavior in a teenager who is rebelling. The teen has finally reached an age where striking out on his own just might be feasible. So it feels safer to threaten his position in the family unit because he's growing more independent.

And when we find ourselves rebelling as adults, it just might be because we feel Life (or others) imposing too many rules on us, and we want to burst free from the limitations of those rules. Rules have power. Power to protect us, and power to restrict or constrain us. If we have any degree of the victim left in us, if we feel that we're still not taking full responsibility for ourselves, it might be because…

… Growing up means having power.

We've seen power misused, and we don't want to walk in those footsteps. It's like when I was a young teen, I thought I would become a teacher. But then the high school teachers went on an extended strike, and some students weren't able to graduate and go on to college. As much as I wanted to sympathize with the underpaid teachers, I wanted nothing to do with a group who would put more importance on making more money than protecting the students who were in their charge. Admittedly, I was pretty young at the time, but that was the judgment I made.

Similarly, if being an adult is fraught with negative associations, associations we made when extremely young, even as young as Jason's first years, we will find ways to continue to be a victim, self-sabotage our efforts at success to display how unready we are to step into the role fully.

But being a victim means that we are still giving our power away to someone or something else. And we continue the cycle of blaming the other when something doesn't work out for us, looking for the next person or situation to which we give our power.

Taking responsibility means we have to redefine what power means to us. We have to acknowledge that we can redefine our entire belief system around power because there are plenty of examples of adults who display beautiful use of their power and are able to help others because of it. We have to recognize that what we saw as an abuse of power might have been an inability of the other person to wield that power wisely, or simply an insufficient amount of knowledge or experience in the role they had.

Now it's time to look at Aaron, the first three-year-old boy. What I felt from him was that he still hadn't decided how he felt about this strange world, and he was choosing to sit back and observe for a while. Loved as he was, if he was allowed to have many experiences without being pressured to conform to the standards of development as defined my modern science, then he would decide when he was ready to come forth, and everything would be fine. He waved at me as I left, a new occurrence for him towards a complete stranger.

What these two boys teach us is that it's up to us to decide when we are ready to move forward, to take the next step in our lives. At the same time, it's important to see if our reluctance to do so is due to our negative perception about power, or if we are rebelling against something.

To the Rescue!

From a very early age, we hear many stories of rescue. Fairy tale heroines are rescued by the heroes. Our parents rescue us when we get into trouble in our young lives. The entire premise of the insurance industry is to rescue us from unforeseen events. The same is true with the medical establishment that rescues us from accidents and from the effects of our not following a recommended lifestyle; for example, we hope a pill will magically make us thin. We follow a stock tip and project onto it the power to make us rich! Our government establishes safety nets for a variety of emergencies we may experience, from unemployment to social security. Even our Creator rescues us from the events of this life by way of Heaven. And sometimes we are rescued by the end of an event, "saved by the bell" as it were.

What all this leads to is an undercurrent of hoping we'll be rescued at some point if things don't go well. For many, this takes the form of lottery tickets. For others, maybe a relationship will rescue us from loneliness or the enormous responsibility of taking care of all the aspects of life by ourselves.

There are two main consequences of this unconscious hope of being rescued. The first is that we give away at least some of our power to this hope. Without even knowing it, we may neglect making decisions and taking action that would move us towards a solution. We lean more toward the victim side and less toward the empowered side.

The second main consequence is that we could find ourselves feeling quite betrayed if we need this rescue and it doesn't come forth. It's again a case of believing that things should work a certain way, and when they don't, we can feel frustrated and "not chosen" for such a gift.

It's important to recognize this possible pitfall, and realize that most of us are far more resourceful than we think. If we take the responsibility for working our own way out of a situation, then we actually get a surge of energy. The determination to take as much control of the situation as we can has the ability to spur us onward, creating momentum.

It takes courage to accept real responsibility for ourselves, but once we step into this arena, new possibilities open up to us. Yes, it will mean more work. It requires us to be able to answer to ourselves for any action we take. It opens us up to a kind of worry that we are not fully equipped to take on this new role. But the power is within us. Regardless of our circumstances, we can choose to believe in a solution. Miracles have taken place when people own their own power, such as with Gandhi's reclaiming his country from foreign rule with no weapons.

Power can come in many forms. Food has the ability to give us health and pleasure, and abuse of food will probably lead to illness. Power is the same— exercised with care, it can bring about enormous benefits. We get to choose.

And choose we should. The more we know about where our behavior comes from, the more we can take back the power that is truly ours. The more we can trust that we will act in accordance to what is here now, rather than respond based on past events, the more we can trust our readiness. And trust is what we need to grow, to erase the ill effects of the betrayal we have suffered, whether actual or perceived.

We have the power to do this. We have the power to choose, and to choose wisely. We have the power to decide when a rule can be relaxed or disregarded altogether, such as eating that piece of cake after all! We have the power to reclaim our freedom.

Let's do this together, and see what kind of tomorrow we make.

OK, can we go now? Please?

<u>Notes</u>

<u>Notes</u>

Notes

<u>Notes</u>

Notes

ABOUT THE AUTHOR

Hélène Patry was a high-tech professional for 20 years, mainly in sales and project management. Due to worsening health issues, she resigned from the corporate world and pursued the study of Energy Medicine. This led her to understand that the body reflects what is going on in the mind, which can defy medical diagnosis.

While getting to the root of her own symptoms, she was also able to assist others through 10 years of conducting sessions. Her store of practical advice and understanding of why people act the way they do has helped many in identifying the cause of, and then the solution to, their issues. Her goal is to propose the shortest possible path to a healthy and joyful life, free from the holds of the past.

An Author, Speaker and Consultant, she now resides in Phoenix, Arizona.

www.ingramcontent.com/pod-product-compliance
Lightning Source LLC
Chambersburg PA
CBHW060427290526
45791CB00002B/886

* 9 7 8 1 5 1 5 3 3 1 6 7 4 *